She Alone

JOHN MENAGHAN

salmonpoetry

Published in 2006 by
Salmon Poetry,
Cliffs of Moher, County Clare, Ireland
Website: www.salmonpoetry.com
email: info@salmonpoetry.com

ISBN 1-903392-56-X

Cover artwork by Peter Voorn
Cover Design & Typesetting: Siobhán Hutson

In memory of my mother
Grace Regina Galvin Menaghan
(1911–2000)

Author's Note

This book-length sequence began with a single poem about a woman reflecting on her life. Over the ensuing months and years I found myself writing, involuntarily as it were, more and more poems about this woman. During a reading in Dublin's Temple Bar in the summer of 2004, I observed: "I'm writing a series of poems about an imaginary woman. I don't know who she is exactly, but she knows who I am, and she knows where I live, because she keeps knocking on my door, saying: 'Time to write another poem about me.' So I do."

Gradually it became clear to me that these poems were beginning to form themselves into an array of perspectives on this woman's life. One important step in that process consisted in my colleague John Reilly's decision to direct a dramatic performance, in April 2004, by actors Lyndsay Kane and Angela Naut, of a selection of poems from the still evolving manuscript. That experience taught me a number of valuable things, but perhaps chief among them was that the decision I (or perhaps the imaginary woman herself?) had made that the poems should not be monologues but third-person poems about her meant that they were neither from the woman's point of view nor from mine but could instead be understood, as both the actors and director understood them, not only as poems in a diversity of forms and styles but as poems embodying diverse voices and perspectives exhibiting varying degrees of sympathy and judgment, and that two or more voices could even be understood to be speaking different parts of the same poem, sometimes to themselves, or to one another, or to some unseen auditor or audience.

As the remark I made to the crowd in Dublin suggests, I found myself in the middle of writing this book before I knew it was going to be one. Even so, an important step in the process of completing it involved not only the dramatic performance mentioned above but also my own reading of some of these poems in public and my sharing portions of the MS. with a number of women of varying ages and temperaments. Each of these gestures or ventures filled me with a sensible degree of trepidation, but the enthusiastic reaction of the women who attended the dramatic performance, as well as of the women who have heard me read one or more of the poems or have themselves read portions of the manuscript, has gone a long way toward giving me the confidence to pursue the project to completion. To all of these women, and to the many others over the years who have helped me to understand, to whatever limited extent, some aspect of their own experience as women in the modern world, I wish to express my heartfelt gratitude.

In addition, I wish to thank Michael Engh, S.J., Dean of the Bellarmine College Of Liberal Arts, Loyola Marymount University, and the College Fellowship Committee for a Fall 2005 College Fellowship providing crucial support that made it possible for me to focus on completing the manuscript; David Killoran, Chair, and the LMU English Department for support of the aforementioned performance at the McIntosh Center, Loyola Marymount University, April 2004; the Bedlam Writers' Group— Phyl O'Connor, Joe Kane, Aidan Hayes, Mary McNelis, & Claire O'Donnell—in Gortahork, County Donegal for providing the stimulating and nurturing context in which the first of these poems began to take shape; Rebecca Cantor, whose research in support of and perspective on the project helped me to move it toward its final shape; and last but definitely not least, Jessie Lendennie, for whose early and continuing support of this project and tireless work on behalf of poetry and poets I cannot even begin to express my appreciation, admiration, and gratitude.

Contents

what? . . who? . . no! . . she! . . SHE!

—Samuel Beckett

Still

What kind of child
turns into her
she couldn't say
for sure only
she did remember
one day when
bright sun lit
up the lawn all
afternoon as
she lay on
the park grass
wanting only
this no longing
to get older
wiser more mature
accomplished just
stay warm on dry
grass under summer
sun and all the cool
nights when a winter
storm beyond her
window made her
think how lucky
to be snug in bed
forever staying
still struck her
as exquisite bliss
movement could
only make things
worse more
complicated
but alone and
motionless in

sun or stormy
dark what could
be better why
grow up at all
when all she
needed was to lie
so still the sun
the sky the dark
the storm the lawn
the bed would never
change never become
just be and she
remain this child
content to lie
still as the world
revolved so slowly
imperceptibly it
seemed the world
too wanted only
to be whirling
always and
forever still.

Girl Talk

for Lucy na gruaige fada

In summer she wandered barefoot to the town's
soft edge and climbed a fence into pasture land
where off in the distance cows nuzzled grass.
If she sat very still and waited, they
would come: a leisurely, lumbering, loose
circle of flesh drawing nearer, tighter
like a slow-closing net as they advanced.
With blinking eyes large as her tiny fists
they regarded her, half disbelieving
what they saw. Closer and closer they came,
tighter and tighter the net, till she felt
afraid a little, but only a little.
When one of the ladies at last let a
tongue drop sloppily from its greedy mouth
and started to lick the soles of her feet,
she discovered, each time anew as if
it were the first, how rough were those wet pink
tongues, yet how infinitely gentle were
these simple creatures the big world called beasts.

Sleep

Whatever else she loved she loved to sleep.
Her mother marvelled how she heard no peep
all the long summer morning until noon.
The neighbour children knocking boldly on
the back door to ask could she come and play.
Her mother answering quaintly: "She's away."
"Away where?" the more curious would try.
"In dreamland," came her mother's soft reply.
She wasn't, though, and yet when Mother checked
she shut her eyes tight, striving to protect
this drifting back and forth, this half and half,
struggling to keep her body still, not laugh
or smile even as her mother stood
to see if she might stir. She understood.
Her mother found such sleep unsettling.
But she found in it refuge from the thing
she feared that had no name yet everywhere
she went it followed (or preceded?) her.
If she fooled Mother could she fool as well
this other she feared might be her true self?
This one not gentle, good, obedient, kind
but bent on badness, with an evil mind
pursuing all the things that were forbid.
It seemed to her that if she somehow hid
her waking from this other she might thrive,
be all the best things that she felt inside
she wanted most to be. Yet always time
kept moving till at last she had to climb
up out of sleep, awake, arise, endure
another day of evil haunting her
and tempting her to the abyss' edge,
quite irresistible though she might pledge
herself to virtue, goodness, happiness.
Her half-sleep sweet; her waking life a mess.

Average

Never a victim.
Never a victor.
Always and only
she gravitates
to middle ground.
Never in first place.
Never in last.
She's always just
hanging around.
No medals.
No booby prizes.
Never the dunce cap.
Never the crown.

Lower Education

She wasn't the girl
the big nun threw
still sitting in her
desk halfway across
the room but
it hardly mattered
when the desk
clattered against
the snot green
wall and the
girl's orange
head well anyway
red took one
second more
before it dribbled
down the wall
like a basketball
followed by a
delicate shower
of paint petals
red-haired Rita
Karina always in
trouble not like
her but still it
was the same
almost as if
she herself had
been sent sailing
as if her skull
too bounced
twice one split
second before
the desk came

crashing down
on cracked grey
tiles so that
crash and crack
were one almost
one sound and her
grimace too matched
Rita's so perfectly
she winced in unison
with that hapless
troubled girl she'd
scarcely ever spoken
to who'd pushed
Sister Angela too
far and paid the
price Rita deserved
that Sister Angela
declared but even
she looked shocked
at what she'd done
with no way to
undo it all act
impact lesson for
the day don't
mess with Sister
Angela she didn't
need to be told
twice or even
once though Rita
for her part
absorbed the shock
but seemed to miss
the point at least

she failed to change
her wild ways though
Sister sort of did
confined herself
for what was left
of their last year
in grammar school
to slapping Rita's
pale cheek blotchy
red with manly
meaty hands that
held both desk
and girl up
to her chest
that day then
threw them hard
against the far wall
while they all but
she especially
looked on in fear
and wonder as
poor Rita crashed
and fell her bright
mane burning blood
and learned from
this as from
most other lessons
Sister taught
nothing at all.

Learning to Skate

A pond at dawn. Mist drifting through bare limbs.
Skates laced tight over triple socks. Gloved hands
shielded from air and ice and sudden spills.
Hard habits to break: wanting to walk
on thin blades, cross her legs, shuffle her feet.
But on this empty pond, with dim, sparse sun
beams peeking through December sky, a soft
snow dropping—soundless, swift—no one in sight,
she pushes off and glides to middle ice.
No way now back to land but on these blades,
or on her hands and knees. She dares herself
the distance to the bank, moves landward, drops
into deep ruts, stumbles, sprawls flat on her back.

There's no one there to laugh, though, but herself,
so gracefully as ice allows she'll rise,
push one bladed foot against grey glass
and show up six thrusts later at the shore.
Emboldened now, she'll ring the pond's hard edge
one full time round, twirl, pivot, slide and race,
blade-dancing, chase gold medals in her mind,
improvise a ballet, get perfect tens,
retire in glory, ankles aching, build
a small blaze at the pond's edge with some scraps,
loosen her laces, shed her snow-soaked gloves,
crouch by the fire as it catches flame,
sending her grin across the rutted gleam
of glassy, fearsome, flame-lit, mastered ice.

Only Child

I.

Somewhere in childhood everything changed.
All talk of brothers, sisters ended then.
Her parents, growing what they called estranged,
said they might separate, but never when
or for how long or why or who'd take care
of her, or one another. Then remained
together in that house, and yet not quite.
And tended to her in between their fights
but didn't seem to care in the same way.
And after years of not quite being there
her father one day truly disappeared.
Her mother turned not to her but away.
She moved, bereft, through lonely nights and days
wondering what she had done or failed to do,
and out of all they'd said which parts were true.

II.

What did the womb remember of its cargo?
The phallus of its thrust? How did her father
parry suggestions that he ought to be
responsible for one brief moment's pleasure
with someone he no longer loved or cared for?
How could her once sweet mother be devoted
to home and garden but treat her own daughter
like some dull burden she must carry with her
until an adult grew from what they'd planted?
She asked herself—but never them—these questions,
until the time came when she moved past caring,
drifting away as they had from each other,
searching for love—or if not love, a lover.

Intimate Acquaintance

Treating herself
like a phone
booth she'd
let anyone
get into
would if
she could
collect an
intimate
crowd
the hollow
buzzing
bell of her
entreaties
echoing in
the street
corner glow
of so many
unanswered
calls.

Possessed

O she knew
don't doubt it
for a second
knew what she
was supposed to
feel to want
only she didn't
not for one
moment try as
she might it
never felt right
be independent
self-sufficient
self-actualizing
they all said
a new woman
who doesn't
need a man to
fulfill her that
wasn't at all
what she wanted
a man for she
wanted love and
babies maybe
nights when no
word need be
said all understood
between them not
self-validation not
some affirmation of
her identity what
identity would she
have when all

was done and
so much left
unsaid what inner
resource would she
call upon when
death came on
would she say
look at me death
and despair you
can't get me can't
you see I'm way
too self-possessed.

No Matter

It was to her
a matter of
no matter.
What did she
want to do?
What work,
they meant.
None, or any.
Nothing spoke
to her, called
her name, declared
designs upon her.
She did this, that,
another thing
besides, all to
get by, that's
all. Work was
work. Profession?
She had nothing
to profess, confess,
redress, express.
Career? In this
sense only: going
downhill fast and
furious. To do?
Her whole life
a to-do list, items
crossed off without
relief or satisfaction
at a job well done.
Just done, yet never
done, of course,
for always more
to do. And if she
didn't ever get done,
well, no matter.

Odd

There must be some reason to care.
The reason was never quite clear.
She tried very hard not to lie,
but the truth bored her to tears.

She never had much cash
yet knew what each thing cost.
Finding her first gray hair
she plucked it and winced at the loss.

She'd lie in the sun like a stone
till her flesh had begun to fry.
Then stare at the stars and long
to float in that cold dark sky.

When her heart filled with despair
people said she was looking her best.
When her body pulsed with joy
her soul craved eternal rest.

She was odd, they all agreed.
Warped in the womb, one said.
Did she even know what that meant?
Would she know once she was dead?

Damn

Again last
night she
dreamt she'd
died but
hadn't yet
made tracks
for heaven
when a frail
voice cried
the next
train doesn't
leave until
until wait
now she
took it
down no
train until
—eternity?

Nothing Doing

It's not that she has nothing to do.
It's that there's nothing she has to do.
It's not that there's nothing for her to do.
It's that all her doing comes to nothing.

Not One

She tried
all the gods
one by one
and together
found they
all failed
to succour
or guide
her make
her holy
whole body
and soul
one by one
hoping for
one that's
all to return
her call collect
her welcome
her shepherd
her lead her
down some
path or smite
her punish her
presumption
blindness vanity
desire redeem
her sins such
as they were
but found only
in the end of all
there was nothing
to embrace bow
down before

appease pray
to ignore reject
defy just earth
and sky no gods
for her not one
or many no
divine plan
just for her
no god at all.

Patience

for Jennifer

Does the flower bloom
under the sun's surly
hurrying eye or simply
because it is time?

Can all her restless
urgent human longings
move the moon one
single inch out of its orbit?

If time ran in reverse
and she waited instead
for things to un-happen,
would her eagerness,
her desire be any less?

What is the world but
a dream from which
she hopes in vain
never to awaken,
a place in the end
she simply can't abide?

What is her future
but a chain of moments
straining then breaking
until she at last understands
the grave import of that
phrase she so often repeated:
so long, so long, why
must it take so long?

She Thinks About Death

no seeing no being
no taste no waste no
hearing no fearing no
lying no trying no pain no
gain no striving no jiving
no smelling no telling
no feeling no reeling
no call no fall no
walk no talk no
time no rhyme
no dream no
scheme no
breath no
strife no
life just
death

Intuition

Foreseeing all, she knew he would depart.
She sees the ends of things before they start.
Resisting every vision till the day
Comes when she can't, and all doubts fade away.

To know all proves less lovely than it might.
Like staring at bright noon and seeing night.
Still, some things come out well enough to say
Darkness is doomed to yield to the new day.

So each sad time of parting too will pass.
Give way perhaps to love that lasts and lasts?
Such second sight might banish all heartaches,
But her heart pays no heed until it breaks.

Busy Body

She didn't always do
what she intended but
always she did some
thing—or else not.
And busy, idle or
somewhere between
those sweet extremes,
mostly she gave a deal
more than she got.

Insomniac

To have no thought
she fears to entertain.
No inner room where
spectres, waiting, stare.
To dream no dream in
half-light, half awake.
No vision that descends
like destiny to crowd
her rest, to corner
every lie sent out
from lips agape
in horror, sleep.
Mouth like a womb:
deep penetrable dark.
Butterfly fluttering
high up in her throat.
To feel preserved,
perfected, understood.
For this she waits.
Meanwhile the world
unravels. Beneath
her breast a bloody
time clock ticks.

Circles

She would if she could find a way of living
which was at the same time a way of dying.
The two combined into a sort of progress
that seemed exquisite stillness from a distance.
Such stillness as resembled, viewed up close,
furious molecules pacing tiny cells.

She would if she could make plans as if she had
not merely world enough and time but means
to stitch the border of sweet, simple days
with threads of chaos, complex and ornate.

She would if she could move through endless circles,
enclosed completely in each moment's sphere,
watching the next advance, the last receding
(memory's frail smoke-ring fading fast)
till she at length became the very air
into which all her moments had dissolved . . .

Discipline

She could discipline her body
from the day's very start,
and train her mind to be
each moment sharp and smart,
but what was she to do
with her wayward heart?

Weathering

Their talk commences
over clattering rain.
Her clothes soaked,
face streaming rivulets.
The towel he hands her
holds his scent, dabbed
to flesh and gently,
firmly pressed, stirring
memories like ancient
murmuring beasts, beautiful
but dangerous. He speaks
his need for solitude, then
reaches toward her, then
withdraws. The air is vast
between them. She cannot
tell him anything. What
he knows he knows. Things
seem to happen without her
approval, as they agree to
independence, inattention,
infrequency. In means
she's out. And so she
exits into storm, zigzags
across his lawn, beats
a rainblind retreat past
tattered trees. He waves
on the threshold, sends
her a distant, faint,
consoling smile. Tears
mingling now with rain,
and now no memory, touch
or scent can comfort her.
Ahead an agony of pointless
days and nothing but time
to tell when all this ends.

Single

O god, no cat!
O please, not that!

Party

A room full of people
if she saw any one
of them again it
would be too soon.

Headphones

Music more soothing
than silence warming
her skin like a quilt.
Brain bones and flesh
expire expand embrace.

The house's quotidian
sounds as good as gone.
Appliances humming
only to themselves.
The muted forlorn

rasp of a telephone.
Muffled t.v. screen
blaring at other ears.
Lightseeds cast sown
scattered into dark.

Just as her mind
drifts off begins
to roam sweet distant
realms a thin hissing
needle pricks her home.

Her arm lifts an arm.
Her frame rises up to
its full height. She
takes her quiet place
within a world of noise.

Difficult

Too smart for her
own good, they said.
Too sensitive besides.
Touchy as hell, and
God help you if you
actually made contact,
flesh to flesh. She'd
shriek and flinch
as if your skin ran
current all along
its surface. Hard
to please, on top
of all the rest.
High standards,
she'd have said.
Snobbery, they
declared, inflated
notions of her
flawless taste.

A waste, they all
agreed, for after all
was said and done
she was a looker,
well, attractive
anyway, pretty
as opposed to
beautiful. No
glamour to her,
not a shred, but
most men agreed
if they could keep
her smart mouth shut

just long enough they
wouldn't mind a night
or two with her in bed.
Most women thought
she thought herself
their better, and were
having none of it.

Children, sensing in her
something hidden, some
impulse to joy and play,
approached, but when
they came too close she
smiled and shrank
into herself as if
by rule. More than
she could do to let
go whatever she
grasped so tightly
in some inner fist
even she couldn't
find, never mind
unclench. Such
a troubled child,
adolescent, woman,
all agreed, thinking
her odd, and
sad, but still
intriguing in her
way, a mystery.
And every time
she did whatever
it was pushed

them all away
she tried to stop
herself, change
into what they
wanted her to be,
whatever that was.

That, to her, was
it: the mystery.
How to be other
than she was?
No one explained,
though if they'd
told her she'd have
tried her best, not
shied away from
any labour, pain.
But in the end
she knew that she
was she, whether
she wished or no,
and so would from
her birth to death
remain this difficult
creature secretly
wishing only
to please and
to be pleased.

The Gods

When the wrong
men rejected her
she wept and
wept and wept
that these men
who might have
been right had
proved so wrong.

But when the right
man rejected her—
a man who was
not to be hers
even though
he was right—
she did not weep.
She was angry then.
Not at the man
—O No—but at
the bloody gods.

Her Fate

It seemed her
fate to love
a very few
very much and
always to have
those very few
love her less.

Procrastination

Lacking that
how would
she know
what to
not do
next?

Two Men

Two men only. The rest
distractions, interludes.
Two men, one dead
too young, one married
too much. One who left
too soon, the other never.
His wife, that is, although
he swore he loved her more
than wife and child both.
The dead one loved her
still more and maybe still
even now beyond the world
if that was where he'd fled
who left her longing for
a thing she'd never had,
just dreamed, just beyond
her grasp—as if the world
had meant for it to be,
then changed its mind.
The world's mind?
When she started thinking
that way all was lost,
the slope to madness
steep and slick. Better
to plant her feet and hold
on tight as the hard
earth kept spinning out
her fate. The other one
was always late, such
a struggle to escape his
real life, spend an hour
with her, and never time
enough to choose a life
with her instead. Two men,
just two. The others all
distraction, interlude.

The Meaning of (Her) Life

She scarcely remembered
her birth never mind
conception not to talk
of wherever she'd been
before that what sense
then to ask why she'd
been born or lived to tell
the tale or lack thereof
or why almost nothing
happened and yet her
life went on and on
and on while the only
thing she could be
certain about was
that it wouldn't not
forever anyway and
without that sort of
guarantee how could
she make plans or
take time to ponder
the great mysteries
so she stuck to
the little ones why
only when she tried
too hard did things
really go wrong
why she only lost
things she wanted
to keep why all
she had to give
was never quite
what anyone else
wanted why she
ever even bothered
to ask why.

Hungry

It's not that she's hungry exactly
it's that she's hungry inexactly
in a way no man could ever
understand what would he
know about hating every
morsel she craves or how
trying on clothes means
needing to be brave what
possible conception could
he have of fearing some
well-meaning fool will ask
how pregnant she is when
she hasn't even made love
for so long she's forgotten
what a man famished for
pleasure feels like deep
inside taking his fill of her
only always come and gone
before she even knows which
way is down leaving her not
just high and dry but starving
so thoroughly no food could
ever satisfy no liquor slake
her vicious thirst remembering
all that misspent appetite worse
than the actual moment driving
her not crazy but straight for
the kitchen to smother and
drown going to town on cold
leftovers wanting nothing now
but to be left alone to nourish
herself all the wealth in the world
couldn't buy her off then and

only when she wakes all bloated
and logy the next morning will
she tell herself she'll never again
let go like that and it's true too
because each time she does it's
always a little different important
to learn from the mistakes of
the past she tells herself and
laughs that way she's completely
free in the future to make a
brand new series of mistakes.

Body & Soul

She knows the body rots, but does the soul?
Can something lacking form remain a whole?
Or is soul, being nowhere, everywhere
her body's ever been, filling each hole
left by the body when it moves along?
A lack in the place of a shape? Silence
where song had one time sounded loud and long?
She only knows some voice inside her says
this world cannot be all, and longs to learn
a realm exists where her—and every—soul
endures beyond decay. But still she fears
when body's laid in ground or burned away
the soul falls into—if not pieces, peace—
a deathly calm, as if it never were.
Or truly never was, and that faint voice
whispering within an empty cavity
tells nothing but the body's deep desire
to find itself immortal after all.

Foresight

Had she been
a little less
careful she might
never have missed
nearly as much
as she planned.

Finding Her Way

What she longs to find,
what she's yet to discover
is a way into the day
and then a way thru it,
her own, not shaped by
circumstance or duty,
in which each moment
to moment movement
happens as smoothly,
naturally, pleasantly
as her most happy,
harmonious moments,
a string of such moments
lengthening thru the day,
like saying her own daily
rosary, celebrating her
own and the world's
mysteries—sorrowful,
joyful, and such—till
sleep comes creeping
over her like a comforter
pulled up to the chin
on a winter's night
and smiling she drifts
into dream, the day
not just over but spent,
well spent, and all night
long lost in shapeless
visions till she wakes
ready to move in
her graceful way
thru another day.

Home

This place suffused not
with spirits but thin traces
gaunt remains of deeds
done words spoken or left
unsaid undone undoes her
now all these years later
coming back to find she
has no home not even one
away from home no firm
connection to the earth no
place that calls her back
and says abide here you
will thrive and feel fully
alive don't look back or
so the wisdom goes and
maybe it's always folly
this effort to visit a past
life situation context lost
dissolved surrendered at
the border to some newer
world so many years ago
some lustrous future once
her future till it too grew
old became no more than
just another past she'll
try to visit someday and
discover it too lies beyond
her grasp teasing her with
dangled shards of fact
fragments of circumstance
so many places where she
once existed still exist
themselves after a fashion
still remain but do not
know her name.

Missing Her Period

After it went, the power to conceive
and bring flesh of her flesh into the world,
each new day's light and warmth seemed like a cloak
she pulled up to her chin to ward off chills
even as brushfires singed her face and frame.

The grave's grey cold and furnace's red heat
competed to drive home her slow return
to ash or clay, the road she must go down
with no survivor to leave in her wake
or help her on her journey to the end.

She found herself then longing for the pain,
cramps that had laid her low so many days,
the dripping blood, potential's slow discharge,
expulsion from the deep, edenic womb
signaling loss and freedom both at once.

The curse, the chance, the choice forever gone
like so much else the stealthy years purloined
while she dreamt what might happen. And what had?
Her life, the "best" part, so the others claimed.
Free now forever from that burden, hope,

temptation, threat, capacity and power,
she missed it terribly, and each night longed,
as in her childhood, to feel complete,
and feel her body pulsing like some sun
pregnant with endless possibilities.

When She Was Young

When she was young
she often felt alone in
her thoughts and feelings.
And she hoped when
she got older she would
find people with whom
she could connect, with
whom she could share.
One person especially.
And she did find people.
And thought at times
she had found that one
person. But here she
found herself, after
all the years, alone.
Alone as she'd ever
been. Maybe more.
And the possibility
presented itself quite
forcefully that she
might well remain
alone, until she died.
At that cold thought
a winter chill moved
through her and all
at once she saw her
body lying all alone
in the frozen ground.
Then life—not death
but life—seemed
to her at last what
it had seemed at first,
when she was young,
a mystery more strange
than words could tell.

Things

The way in
the beginning
there were
just things
she did
and things
she didn't

but one day
it all turned
into a life
she had
allegedly
chosen
to live.

She Alone

She alone
has known
the dreams
that haunt
her brain
particular
as pain
whose prick
never quite
fades all
that remains
after acute
visions have
fled. She
alone has
stood upon
thin shores
as brown
hills blurred
to black
then vanished
into darkness
night on night.
She alone
has wandered
city streets
as false
dawn broke
upon her
shoulders
bent down
by delicate
burdens deep

reluctance
to emerge
from dark
and suffer
sun's assault.
Nobody's fault
and yet no
matter what
she did
embraced her
solitude sought
connection or
patiently waited
to be found
by one who
wanted all
she had to
offer offered
freely if not
openly to
he who
knew enough
to want and
ask for it
and offer
back his
all to her
after all
that this
was all
there was
from all
her effort

no effect
all she was
always left
bereft and
all she
suffered
all she had
to hold no
one ever
quite there
beside her
though close
by or on
or in her
even no true
union no
connection no
companion no
one else just
she alone.

Enough

Well, it was enough,
wasn't it, to live
no matter what
happened or didn't.
So what if she
never became some
female Picasso, never
met—or anyway
married—the right
man, had beautiful,
talented children
devoted to her
in old age, or
even one lifelong
friend, never really
got along with her
parents, relations,
co-workers at
a series of silly
jobs, never found
the perfect place
to live. Enough
to live at all.
And if she was
at times, well,
just a little
disappointed,
at times, she
had to admit,
just a little
defeated by
circumstance,
well, so what?

Wasn't she still
alive? And even
if that didn't mean
all things were
possible, well,
some things were,
surely? And wasn't
that, if only just,
enough?

What She Wanted

She wanted to paint
and she has painted
but too little.

She wanted to wander
and she has wandered
but too little.

She wanted to dream
and she has dreamed
but too little.

She wanted to love & be loved
and she has loved & been loved
but too little.

She wanted to live
and she has lived
but too little.

She never wanted to die
yet she has died
little by little.

Efficiency

Whatever she plans to do
she doesn't
at least not in the way or at the time
she'd planned.

What if she planned to do nothing
from now on?
It might in the end be the best way
to get things done.

The Visitation

One day they just appeared—the Mother, Father.
And all that she could think was: Well, why bother?
Where were they when she needed them the most?
Who wanted to commune with two old ghosts?

Still Born

Although her child never saw daylight
he was still born and lived within her mind.
She never told another soul the truth:
that he had never died for her at all.
From infancy to childhood to pimpled
adolescent angst she saw him through.
What could she do but love him when he chose
his first girlfriend because she looked like Mom,
or when his college major was her own,
and later he became her kind of man?
She watched him grow & grow & choose & choose,
and if sometimes she felt a girl child might
have pleased her more, and if deep down she knew
he'd never even breathed a single breath,
another part of her knew just as well
that he would only really disappear,
only be truly dead at her own death.

All the One

She has done her share of drinking
but the drinking she has done
in the end is all the one:
to forget why she was drinking,
to forget what she was thinking,
to neglect her own concerns,
for she's one who never learns
that the shortest path to sorrow
is to fret about tomorrow
since the wise ones say
tomorrow never comes.
But for all the heed she pays
to such wisdom she might
well be deaf and dumb.
So she drinks instead of thinking
as the evening sun is sinking,
as the daylight's slowly going
for she's all the while knowing
in the end it's all the one:
we're all undone . . .

Through

All she asks now?
To make it
through the day,
die in the night,
peaceful, in sleep.
To live till then
through day and
night without
excess of anguish,
crippling loss
and then to
drift her dust
through worlds
unknown and
never rest
and never
feel alone.

Before

sometimes
          it seemed
               to her
                    she'd been
before the body
         came to call
              pure spirit
                   of some sort
        or if not pure
airy at least
                 and floated
      god knows where
            through realms
(the word itself
       seemed to confer
           upon her
              royal attributes)
       where subtle gestures
untroubled
                 by limb's
          or eye's
      or mouth's
demands
       or
               boundaries
expressed her essence
          partially yet perfectly
      as if the
insubstantial
             evanescent
     were both part
          and whole
      motive
            act

and

outcome

all in one

as if

this being

both

limitless

and self-contained

would never cease

and she remain

afloat

on

possibility

before

betrayed
into a body
she became
some other thing
alone uncertain
moving clumsily
forward and back
and side to side
yet always toward
oblivion her only
hope an inkling
that she might
by losing body
once again
become what
she had been
before

lissome

spirit

nothing

more

Oublier Les Roses

for Peter Voorn, and for Liz Russell

> *There is nothing more difficult for a truly creative painter than*
> *to paint a rose, because before he can do so he must forget all*
> *the roses that were ever painted.*
> —Henri Matisse

> *The real thing is almost impossible to do.*
> —Henry James

> *Rose is a rose is a rose.*
> —Gertrude Stein

I.

Sometimes the paint behaved, and sometimes not.
She had the sense some gesture she'd forgot
to make (imagine) kept not happening
as she tried or tried not to do this thing.

II.

Aphrodite with the Aleph opening,
the golden spear point glistening,
her holy alphabet's first letter.

Ares, Aphrodite, Artemis, Athena, Apollo:
a pentagram of star points, Eros' radiant
arrows departing the deep heart's core.

Swallowcross, middling shafts, inpointing
straight at the heart, the eagle's rest, scorpio,
nest with no next or nexus, death of desire.

Over Delos Aphrodite roams, heart-sore,
pursuing the perfect rose, earthbound Antares
blooming where Artemis & Apollo first arose.

Finding it, would she make
the perfect cut, or let it be,
swaying in wind that once
caressed the distant stars.

Bull and cow, god and goddess,
left to wander over sacred ground.
Taurus tearing through April,
swallowcross laid over star,
vulva and phallus, mystical rose.

III.

Ancient mysteries half understood,
picked up from some mystic artist
she'd met long ago and loved too
briefly, imperfectly, bodies and minds
mixed so unequally that, as Donne
(was it?) declared, such love, though
it flower a moment, soon must die.

Where did all that leave her?
Standing before a canvas, stretching
her heart, her mind to find a medium,
mode, procedure. How to begin?

IV.

Oil. Water. Acrylic. Tempera. Encaustic.
Of what could she be sure beyond
the simple fact she had to choose?
Her hands should have told her which
touched her the most, which medium
she needed to join her soul to other
souls, the tactile dictating the tactics,
but always her mind would doubt
her body, interpose between the fingers
and the feelings, leaving her certain
of nothing beyond the veil of sheer
confusion spilling like a river from
some lofty cliff, leaving her blind.

V.

Gesso and her
best guess how
to ground this
vague conception,
make it flower.

As if she were
pregnant with
something but
scarcely knew
what sort of
creature she'd
conceived.

A child? Some
vegetable love
meant to grow
in other soil?
The spoils
of some raid
she'd made in
dream on worlds
insubstantial as
rain that fades
to vapour as
it falls above
parched earth
drier than
cosmic dust?

VI.

Drying time to consider,
should she ever begin,
way beyond her prime.
Scraping, layering,
surfaces surging
like petals over
thin green stems.

VII.

Figure and ground?
Go figure. Go to
ground. Drive
the vehicle into
the ground and

then figure out
what to do from
there, to free
the goddamned
vehicle from
the ravenous,
greedy ground.

Colours. Pigments.
How would she
ever mix them all
equally, make out
of nothing a rose
that would never
die because it had
never lived, never
been about to be,
never about to
wither, disappear?

VIII.

That "he" nagging,
nibbling at her soul
in spite of herself,
Matisse's remark
just sitting there
in her notebook
all these years
like some unjust
rebuke she can't
quite manage to
dismiss, ignore.

IX.

Line, stroke, texture.
Brush, stick, finger.
Canvas, board, paper.
Her vices, devices,
deceits and despairs.
Details—only that
in the end. Means
that mean nothing,
meant only to move
her from absence,
blankness to a
something there,
a what and a where.

X.

Her whole life's secret mission,
scope, ambition, enterprise:
to find the method, means
and medium, technique,
gesture, grace, restraint
to make it all cohere,
let the rose bloom as
if it fed on azure air.

Till one day, death
looming at the close
of her long road, long
past any hope she'd
harboured that success
might come at last,

forgetting all the roses
she drifted that rainy day
through space and time
as if her hand and body,
canvas, brush, palette,
pigment were all one
and she came closer than
she'd been or hoped to be
to having her flesh flower,
mind and heart and soul
appear before her as one
sweet totality and knew
self-portraiture had been
her whole habit and goal,
and made at last one nearly
perfect painting, perfect rose.

XI.

Nearly. Perhaps. Or not so near as that.
Distance and time informed her all too soon
the rumour of success was premature.
Something wrong or missing. How
to know which or what, or what
to do, change, add, subtract, amend?
The canvas stood in some dim corner
of her mind and room, neglected,
as her days dwindled down to one.

But on that last day, unaware she'd
even risen from her bed, she found
herself before the dusty canvas staring
hard, as if death's secret might lie there.

She found instead a kind of miracle,
the power she had sought till then in vain,
to see life clear and plain, and picked
up tube and palette, squeezed and stroked
not in frenzy but so calmly, quietly she
heard her breath escape, return, felt
her eyes burn as the brush moved
and made mere motion into mystery
till in the end she knew why she had
risen, come, and laboured: it was done.

XII.

And yet as she stepped back to look
something inside her stayed unsatisfied,
and she began to weep instead of smile
and understand at last just where she stood.
She moved back toward the canvas stealthily
as if the blooming rose might turn and run,
and leaned in close and held her breath and gaze,
taking one long last look—and then despaired.

Those last strokes made clear all she might have done.
She seized a blade and slashed till it was gone.
Too late. No time left for her to become.
Time only to play blind and deaf and dumb.

Now

It seems nearly
certain now
that nothing
matters but how
to know that
at the time
it seems somehow
beside the point
to worry over
what didn't happen
but all that
still haunts and
hovers just out
of view as
if it might
still be reality
if only she
knew how to
make it happen
to undo everything
and choose again
only this time
the right things
how would she
know she'd know
she's certain but
so what if
no undoing can
be done her
life her life
all she gets
the one not
enough to get

it right still
can it matter
now no no
not now nothing
matters now not
even the longing
that won't leave
her and yet
leaves her here
all done now
but the things
she would have
done had she
but known alone
she gazes out
over the sea
and thinks how
far she's come
to be nowhere.

After Life

She died as she'd been born: in hope and pain.
Glad for the change, with no urge to remain,
go back to where she'd been, be born again.

What she had done or not done all gone by.
What she had wanted, gotten, lost and why
she'd cared, for whom, obscured in the dim sky

that hovered overhead as her eyes closed.
And yet she smiled a sec, wrinkled her nose
remembering the day a single rose

had made her happy, hopeful, full of life,
made her believe she'd be somebody's wife.
And then again remembering like a knife

plunged through her adolescent breast the pain
when thinking she would paint her way to fame
some teacher told her No. She had no claim

to greatness. No point striving. All she'd do
was waste her life, no talent and no clue.
Then one last breath released that anguish too,

the dreams, the doubts, the struggle to be free
and yet connected, the desire to be
all to someone, through joy and misery.

Only to find herself always alone.
A place to stay but never quite a home.
Time now to see what else might be to come.

Looking Back

From here beyond the view is not so bad.
Death's like the pied-à-terre she never had.
Life seems to rhyme, though this too may be dream.
But being's no issue now. Enough to seem.
Enough, as she'd suspected all along.
The trying's all, the singing of the song.
No matter if the voice be cracked and hoarse.
No matter, so the music take its course.
Death's no crescendo either, it turns out.
If Life's a long slow song, what's Death? A shout
that echoes through eternity, she hopes.
If not, well, as she did in life, she'll cope.

Once

She
used
to be
she did
it's true
gone now
vanished
leaving
behind
no trace
no clue
no mark
no impact
memory
in minds
or hearts
mourning
her loss
no heir
no legacy
nothing left
or right
or down
or up
but she
was here
once every
day each
breath she
took was
hers alone
until the
last one

out not in
all over then
as if she
herself had
never been
herself had
never breathed
at all had never
held a mirror up
and seen a face
her own and
no one else's
looking back
then fogged
the glass with
vapour put that
mirror back
down on her
vanity and
when it
cleared
not just
her breath
but very
self had
disappeared.